Golf Basics for Beginners

The Ultimate Guide about Clubs, Etiquette, Equipment, History and Terminology

Aaron Knight

This book is dedicated to my wife who encourages me to pursue and enjoy my passions without guilt. This book would have never happened without your love and support.

Ordering Information:
Quantity sales; Special discounts are available on quantity purchases by corporations, associations, and others. For details, contact the "Special Sales Department" at the address above.

-- 1st edition

Manufactured in the United States of America

TABLE OF CONTENTS

PUBLISHER'S NOTES

Disclaimer

This publication is intended to provide helpful and informative material. It is not intended to diagnose, treat, cure, or prevent any health problem or condition, nor is intended to replace the advice of a physician. No action should be taken solely on the contents of this book. Always consult your physician or qualified health-care professional on any matters regarding your health and before adopting any suggestions in this book or drawing inferences from it.

The author and publisher specifically disclaim all responsibility for any liability, loss or risk, personal or otherwise, which is incurred as a consequence, directly or indirectly, from the use or application of any contents of this book.

Any and all product names referenced within this book are the trademarks of their respective owners. None of these owners have sponsored, authorized, endorsed, or approved this book.

Always read all information provided by the manufacturers' product labels before using their products. The author and publisher are not responsible for claims made by manufacturers.

Print Edition 2014

CHAPTER 1: THE DEBATABLE AND INTERESTING HISTORY OF GOLF

The history of golf originated about five centuries ago. Because golf was a distraction for other combat drills, it was banned by James II of Scotland on March 6, 1457. Both sports fans and historians tend to agree that the Scottish were the first true fans of golf. But, on the other hand, no one really knows who actually started the game of golf. As a matter of fact, it is still a subject open for debate if you talk to the right people.

It has been said that the game was probably started by sheepherders out of pure boredom. Supposedly, they tried to amuse themselves by hitting round stones into rabbit holes. They used their wooden staffs as a hitting stick. What started as a way to pass away the time quickly changed into a game with a competitive nature. By the fourteenth century, there were different types of golf games played in countries such as France, Holland, Belgium and Scotland. This is why people still don't know which country started the game of golf, and they continue to debate the issue.

It has also been documented that James VI, a Scottish Baron, was the person who introduced the game to the British. In the very beginning, the game of golf was played on a rough surface. There was no need to play on manicured or well maintained grass. During the early times, the game was played on flatland with makeshift holes.

In 1744, a group of Edinburgh golfers were the first to form an actual golf organization. It was called the Honourable Company of Edinburg Golfers. During this time in history, there were 13 rules that were used for annual competitions. The first competition had players from both Ireland and Great Britain.

In 1766, England was the first country to form a golf organization outside of Scotland. It was called the Royal Blackheath Golf Club of England. In 1818, The Old Manchester Golf Club was also formed outside of Scotland on the Kersal Moor.

North American started its first golf clubs, The Quebec Golf Club and The Royal Montreal Club, during the end of the 1800's. Golf became popular in the United States about 1888. John Reid was the first person to build a three-holed golf course in Yonkers, New York, and he was from Scotland. Another area golf club called the St. Andrews Club of Yonkers was located on thirty acres. It was in close proximity to the original three-hole golf club.

Although it had a slow start, golf quickly became one of America's favorite sports. Shinnecock Hills, built in 1891, was a pretty modern golf club during its time. Amazingly, from 1891 to the end of the century, more than one thousand golf clubs were started in North

America.

Golf has very rich historical value. The game has evolved tremendously from being just a little shepherd's game to what it is today. It is hard to believe that it has transformed into a very popular sport that is loved by people from all over the world.

Golf has grown in popularity through the years, and it is still gaining in popularity each and every day. At one point in history, golf was only played by a few privileged people. However, these days, it is a sport that is loved and played by all types of people. This is probably because of celebrities such as Tiger Woods and other well known and likeable golfers who have caught the eye of many people. It fascinates even people who have never played golf before. So it should not surprise anyone that it continues to be a popular game, especially when Hollywood and the media glorifies golfers and makes them heroes.

Both the golf culture and industry have changed through the years. Golf is big business. There are whole communities and resorts that are devoted to golf. It is easy to find a good game of golf because there are plenty of nice golf courses to choose from. This is because more and more golf courses are cropping up every year.

No one really knows what caused golf to be so popular. But, there are so many people who play the game with their parents and grandparents. It is played by generations of people. Also, there are plenty of schools that have golf programs where people can learn how to play golf. If these things are any indication of how popular golf is, then it will continue to be one of the world's favorite pastimes.

Chapter 2: The Importance of Golf Etiquette

Amateurs and professionals alike are expected to behave a certain way from the very moment they step onto the first tee box. Read on to see the rules of etiquette that all golfers are expected to follow.

Rule #1

Always be punctual. Most golf courses don't allow you to just show up and get on the course, with almost all requiring tee time appointments. Try to arrive 30 minutes prior to your schedules time, as this will allow you to warm up, check-in, and take care of cart rentals and other details before you play.

Rule #2

Dress correctly. Every course has a dress code in place that needs to be adhered to. The rules are different from place to place, so call ahead and make sure that you know what they are. Since cell phones have become a standard accessory for most, ask about those, too Some courses do not allow you to take cell phones out with you, while others ask that you turn them off or switch them to vibrate. If in doubt, leave the phone behind.

Rule #3

Before you tee off, have an order of play decided upon and ready to go.

Rule #4

Refrain from talking when someone in yours or another group is about to play a shot. This is especially true when they are putting, which is also when you should be sure to be out of their line of vision.

Rule #5

Pay attention to what's in front of you when you hit. If you think your shot has a chance of landing in or around the group ahead of you, wait until they have moved. The same rules apply with the space behind you. Common sense says that people won't crowd you when you are going to swing, but accidents happen, so check first.

Rule #6

Protect the course. When you are on the green, be sure to repair all ball marks and divots. Take time to rake the sand traps smooth after you have played out of them. When exiting a trap, leave on the shallow side to limit any potential damage.

Rule #7

If you have rented a cart, follow all the rules as to how and where they should be driven. All designated paths and drivable areas will be clearly marked, but be aware that these can change on days when rain becomes a factor.

Rule #8

Hollywood has done a great job of making you believe that major business deals can be made or broken on the golf course, but that is seldom true. It takes concentration to play the game, so don't break that, saving all business talk for the club house.

Another common theme shown is betting on the outcome of the game, or even a single hole. If you need to do that, keep it to a minimum so that the game retains its fun qualities.

Rule #9

If you are playing at a course where a caddy is provided for you, always remember to tip. If you are unsure what the amount should be, ask one of the course regulars.

Rule #10

Relax and have fun!

GOLF TERMINOLOGY EXPLAINED

It doesn't matter how long you have been playing the game, there is always a chance that some new terminology will be used that you are unaware of. You have a couple of options when this happens: smile and nod like you know the meaning of the new word or phrase, or ask what it means. The latter option is always the best.

Even if you know little about golf, words like bogey, birdie, and slice are ones that you probably know. That may not be the case with balata, which just so happens to be the rubbery material covering the ball. Here are a few lesser known terms you might come across.

If you hit the ground well behind the ball, that is referred to as a chunk. The word is used in reference to the large divot of grass that gets thrown up, and which usually ends up going a greater distance than the ball. The same type of shot, done intentionally, in a bunker is referred to as an explosion. If the ball is buried deep in the sand trap, feel free to call it a fried egg.

If you swing and hit high on the ball, it is called a top shot. This usually happens when you are trying to over compensate for the large number of chunks in your previous shots. A top shot will result in the ball having almost zero loft, which is not good news when you are in a sand trap. In fact, a top shot in a bunker usually means fried egg time.

If you are playing a casual round of golf with friends, you might all agree on a set number of Mulligan's. Those are essentially the same as a "do over" and can be applied when you have hit a particularly appalling shot. Once you have reached the set number of Mulligan's for the day, you are out of luck after that point.

Golfers that find it impossible to putt with a smooth, steady stroke may have developed a case of the yips. The swing becomes jerky, sending the ball off in all directions except the right one.

How you step up to the ball is known as the address. Professional golfers are aware that USGA rules state that the address has taken place the moment the club is rested on the ground behind the ball.

Those who aren't ready to make the step to the pro level can compete using the Nassau method. That means having a score for the front nine, the back nine, and the full 18 holes. The three different scores increase the chances of the golfer winning at least once during the course of the day.

Other terms you might hear include the grain, which is the angle of the grass. The loft refers to the face of the club, while a dormie tells you that the person with the lowest score in the group has reached a point where a tie is his best option.

You don't have to learn the terminology in order to have fun playing golf, but there is no denying that it does help a little.

CHAPTER 3: GOLF EQUIPMENT

Golf Shoes

You are, as you might imagine, required to wear some type of shoes on your feet when golfing, but is it necessary to go with golf shoes? The answer is one that can only be given by each individual golfer.

The vast majority of courses will require all gofers to wear soft spikes so that the course doesn't get trampled and damaged by the hundreds of feet that walk on it daily. Soft spikes are usually allowed in the clubhouse, too, as they don't do any damage to carpeting.

The question that many have is whether or not golf shoes are necessary to play the game. They really aren't, and what each individual chooses to wear usually comes down to comfort and personal choice. The reality is that footwork is more important to a golfer than footwear.

Good footwork starts with the wearing of comfortable shoes. Uncomfortable shoes can be a major distraction, as well as having the potential to cause painful blisters.

In order to have a consistent swing, you require a certain level of stability. As such, golf shoes may be a good choice for those that plan on playing regularly. That is because the cleats on the bottom of the shoe allow you to maintain a solid footing throughout the swing. That is an incredibly important part of a good swing, as the grip helps you maintain your balance as you swing away.

The most important aspect of the footwear that you choose is comfort. There is already enough to think about when you play without having to constantly focus on what is going on with your shoes.

Golf Bags – A Necessary Expense

A good golf bag has to be on the list of essentials for all golfers. What's great is that there is a wide variety of styles available, meaning that there is a bag out there for everyone.

One of the more popular styles is the bags that have fold out legs. The golfer can then stand the bag up when they play a shot, which means doing away with all off the constant bending over to pick it up. This is invaluable for those golfers that choose to walk the course. There is enough bending that goes on during the course of an average round without adding more bending to pick up the bag after every shot.

Every bag has compartments on the inside where the clubs are then situated. There is no particular way that the clubs have to be sorted, and it is usually down to the golfer how he or she wants the bag to be set up. While some golfers put the clubs in any old way, others are sticklers for organization so that they can quickly grab the club they need without any real thought. Some golf bags come with tubes that are designed to protect the grips of the club. This is a very nice touch, as the tubes can add some real life to the grips.

Another thing to consider when shopping for a golf bag is the number of pockets that it has. You will never hear a golfer state that a bag has too many pockets. If the bag you buy comes with a hood cover, you will need a pocket to hold that while you play. Another pocket is required for all of the towels that you will be carrying. Newcomers to the game are surprised at how important towels are to the game, as they are used to wipe off sweat from your brow and hands. You will also need a pocket for your golf tees and any other tools you might use. Last, but by no means least, you will need a larger pocket to hold all of your golf balls. The average golfer usually has a dozen spare balls in the bag at any given time.

Depending on your skill level and the difficulty of the course, you may need some more balls over and above the dozen you usually carry. It's not unusual for golfers to have an extra box of balls tucked away in yet another pocket in their bag.

Golf Clubs

Many people believe that walking into any gold shop and picking up the first set of clubs they see will prepare them perfectly for a game, but that is not the case. Clubs that are either too long or too short can affect how you play, and can actually cause aches and injury. If you have to spend too much time compensating, you won't be able to play your best game, which often means fun is taken out of the equation.

Getting a great set of clubs does not mean having to spend a small fortune on a custom fit. If you have money to spend, that is one way to go, but any well-stocked golf store should have a set that can fit you without going the custom route. That said there are some things you need to be aware of.

While club length is important, it's not the only thing to consider. Pro golfers will tell you that the size of the grip on the club is important, as is the comfort it provides. You will often see club grips for women and young players being smaller in size.

If you would sooner go with a custom set of golf clubs, there is a definite process that needs to be followed. You can't simply hand over your measurements, as your game will also play a role in the finished clubs. The club needs to reach from the point of your outstretched hand to the ground, but there are other considerations, too.

The person making the clubs will have to take a look at your swing and create the clubs with that in mind, which is not something that comes cheaply.

There are some manufacturers that will make you pay a hefty fee for this fitting, but there are also others that may be willing to do it for free, as long as you promise to purchase their particular brand. Yes, you will pay more for a set of custom gold clubs than you would for those off the rack, but you will reap immediate benefits when you take to the course.

There are countless shots that you have played over the years where you would have to compensate for the club being used. Your height, or lack thereof, as well as muscle weakness can make you struggle with regular clubs. All of that can be addressed when you opt for custom made clubs.

It really does come down to budget and personal choice when selecting clubs. If you have a budget that allows you to buy top quality clubs, you may want to go all out and get a custom set.

Golf Clubs for Lefty-Handed Players

The vast majority of golf clubs on the market are designed for players that have a right-handed shot. Southpaws are often left out when shopping for clubs, but that doesn't mean that golf clubs for the lefty aren't available. If you are left-handed, you may be able to adapt and use right-handed clubs, but most golfers play better when they swing from their natural side.

Any good golf store should have a decent selection of left-handed golf clubs and putter. Many golfers forget about the putter when they buy, but it is essential that you go with a lefty putter if you plan on playing from that side. Failing to do so can lead to confusion and a less than impressive putting game.

The problem that left-handed players are likely to face comes when they want to upgrade individual clubs, as those are a whole lot harder to find in the stores. The same rules don't apply to right-handers, all of whom have a massive selection of clubs to choose from.

The reality is that about 90% of all the world's golfers play right-handed, so it only makes sense that most of the equipment will be made for them. There are companies out there, though, that understand the needs of the lefty, and who make quality products aimed specifically at them.

Consider Going with Pre-Owned Clubs

Getting started in the game of golf can be a pricy affair, which means selecting pre-owned equipment may be something that the average golfer has to consider. The good news is that it's actually quite easy to find quality used equipment at a price that will fit your budget.

The right clubs can really help your game, which makes buying a used set a little bit tougher than buying new. You want to be able to get a set of golf clubs that suit your game, and if you are patient in your search, you can land a great set at an affordable price. There are plenty of used options out there, and you can even find a pre-owned set of left-handed clubs if you really take the time to do a thorough search.

Looking After Your Golf Clubs

It has already been explained how important your clubs are to your game, which is why taking proper care of them is so essential. The simple act of keeping them clean can potentially add years to the life of your golf clubs. The good news is that it really doesn't take much to clean them.

All you need to do is mix some mild dish liquid (do not use dishwasher liquid) into a bucket of water. An old tooth brush can then be used to "scrub" the clubs, while a good supply of dry towels can be used to dry off the freshly cleaned clubs.

The process begins by mixing a few drops of the dish soap in with a bucket of warm water. Mix it up a little so that you get a nice collection of suds. There should really only be enough water in the bucket to cover the club heads, so don't fill it to brimming.

The head of your irons should be immersed in the soapy water and washed off with a cloth. Once they are relatively clean, use the old toothbrush to remove excess dirt from the grooves. Give them another little rinse, and then dry them off.

To get the most out of the rinsing part of the process, consider cleaning your clubs outside so that you have access to the garden hose. If you have a sprayer attachment, you will find that this part of the cleaning process goes by very quickly. Once the rinsing is complete, make sure you do a good job of drying the clubs before putting them back in your golf bag.

You might also consider cleaning shafts and woods with a damp cloth. Make sure to never submerge your woods in water, as this can lead to damage that includes the coloring and the protective coat on the head of the club.

While you are in the cleaning mood, you might as well take care of your bag, too. A simple cleaning of the interior with a damp cloth is generally all that is needed. In order to keep the outside looking clean, give it a wipe down after every round. Don't put the clubs back in the bag until they have all been properly dried.

Getting in the habit of cleaning your clubs and bag after each round will ensure that they remain in tip top shape for an extended period of time.

Golf Carts

You can easily rent an electric golf cart at just about every course in the country. It helps make the game move faster, as well as being a convenient way to get your equipment around the course.

When you are new to the game, your first investment will likely be a manual push and pull cart. These great little carts can take the strain of carrying a heavy bag off of your back and shoulders. You ca very easily get a great manual cart for as little as forty dollars. The more details you add to the cart, the more you can expect to pay.

Similar to what you can do with golf clubs, you can easily pick up a gently used manual golf cart for a very reasonable amount of money.

Golf Balls

You simply can't play the game of golf without using balls. The question that most players have is about which balls are the best.

Like many other aspects of golf equipment, this is a decision that usually comes down to individual tastes, as well as how much money the player has in their golf budget.

You will find many golfers who swear by a single brand, and who will never use anything else. These players believe that the ball they use is an integral part of their game, and they will continually use the same brand over and over, regardless of cost.

There is nothing wrong with that, but some common sense should be applied when choosing a golf ball. Beginners need to ignore all the input they will get on different brands of ball. New player will send an incredible number of balls into the heavy rough and water, which means such things as distance and performance really don't come into play. Price should be the number one factor for new balls. One great way to get in the game on a budget is to purchase a large lot of recycled balls, which are those that were considered, lost, but which have been found, cleaned up, and re-sold.

Don't expect to find a ton of brand balls in this batch, but that really shouldn't be a concern. Your only real concern when starting out is getting your swing down and hitting the ball straight. You will go through dozens of balls as you learn to do this, so buying in bulk and steering clear of pricy brands is the best way to go for the new golfer.

As your game improves and your shots become truer, you should then consider a better grade of ball. This should not be your cue to run to the golf store and load up on the most expensive balls available. Consider your budget and skill level, and then choose accordingly.

Players who frequently slice or top the ball (striking the top of the ball with the club head) can inflict a great deal of damage on the balls that they use. This means that a cheaper brand should be used until those errors are removed from their game.

Practice generally does make perfect, especially in golf. Once you have a reached a higher skill level, you can start think about tinkering with different brands of balls. As well as skill level, golfers should also consider the type of course being played on when choosing the right ball.

Golf Tees

Many golfers don't think that tees are a major part of the game, but they really are. What may come as a surprise is that there are a wide variety of tees on the market, each of which has their own advantages. Long tees allow you to set up the ball high, while short tees are the choice of many when teeing off with an iron. Three-pronged tees are very popular with those that want stability, and are also a favorite of purists, as this was the type of tee that everyone used in the early years of golf.

Golf Gloves

It is not everyone that thinks a golf glove is an essential piece of equipment. The benefit that they provide is that they prevent the club from slipping in less than perfect weather conditions. You have a choice of synthetic or leather when choosing a glove. The leather variety is the more expensive of the two, but it tends to last longer. Make sure the glove fits snugly while still being comfortable to wear.

Golf Gadgets and Accessories

The list of gadgets and accessories available to golfers is virtually endless, thanks in large part to how popular the sport has become. Golfers are always looking for ways to make their game better, which is where these gadgets come into play. The rise in popularity has led manufacturers to create even more gadget and accessories for golfers of all levels. While some of the inventions can help your game quite a bit, there are many more that border on the ridiculous. Let's take a look at some of the more popular options.

If you don't have a driving range nearby and also have a small yard, you can still get in some quality driving practice. Virtual golf is fun, but it doesn't truly match the feel you get from the club striking the ball. Another good option is the limited flight ball. As the name suggests, the ball is designed to not travel very far at all. You place the ball on the tee and swing away as normal, safe in the knowledge that the ball won't leave the backyard. There is also the option of using a driving net, but you'll have to make sure that the ball hits every single time.

Another great practice aid is a putting pad, thanks in large part to the fact that they can be used anywhere. You can have a pad in your office or basement, allowing you to practice any time the mood strikes. You can save some time by choosing a putting pad with a cup that has a ball return.

Technology lovers will get a kick out of a digital scorekeeper. Not only is this device a handy way to keep score as you play, it can also save data from numerous rounds so that you can look back on previous games to see of you are improving.

If properly lining up your shot is a problem, you can use a stencil to mark on your ball the exact spot that needs to be hit. Place the stencil on the ball, place it on the tee, and you have a clear target staring you back in the face when you play.

A metronome is another device that golfers often use to perfect the rhythm of their swing.

There are countless golf gadgets to choose from, but make sure that you spend your money wisely when investing. Some gadgets deliver real benefits for a golfer, while others are nothing more that useless junk. Only buy a gadget if you really feel it can improve your game.

enough golfing advice so that you can play a decent game of golf. Why embarrass yourself out on the golf course when help is available?

If you really want to be a good golfer, then you've most likely been playing the game for a while. No one has to explain to you about getting a coach. But, if you are a beginner, then you probably want a way to improve your game right now. In this case, golf lessons could be very helpful for you.

There are those who claim that taking golf lessons gave them the chance to practice on their own and just concentrate on the game. You probably might not get as much done if you practice on your own. For instance, a professional coach will not let you goof off and talk to friends during a real golf lesson. However, there are those who say that having a golf coach who watches their every move and critiques everything they do is very frustrating. Which scenario fits you? Do you need supervision, or can you work alone? The answer to this will determine whether or not you should get a coach, or whether you should just save your money and practice on your own.

Keep in mind that a coach is there to teach the right way to play golf. This means that he is trying to break bad habits. Even though playing the right way is the ultimate goal, there are some excellent golfers who claim that their bad golfing habits help them win. For instance, your coach may yell at you and say that you need to adjust your stance, change your grip or even use a different piece of golfing equipment. But, do you really have to listen to him? Basically, you have two choices. You can do as he says, or you can tell him that your bad habits are advantageous to your golf game. If you aren't going to follow the advice of the golfing coach, should you really be taking golfing lessons? Why waste your money, his time and your time if you are not going to listen to him?

What it boils down to is that taking golf lessons is good for some people, but not for others. You have to decide if lessons will be advantageous for you. But, keep in mind that you can probably get the best results if you just knuckle down and practice.

Internet Golf Lessons?

There are many different avenues for taking golf lessons, and there are many different ways to get the information that you need. Taking golf lessons via the internet is one of the quickest and most efficient ways to learn all about golf. Do you want to get better at golf? Then, try online golf lessons. That's reason enough to at least try them. Right?

It is easy to find decent online golf lessons. The web has tons of good websites what offer golfing lessons. You can even get pointers on how to improve certain parts of your golf game.

You can get good info about how to adjust your stance and follow through on swings. You can also find advanced info about golf swings. Not only can you learn the physical side of golf, but these websites can help you mentally as well. Everyone knows that there is a lot of competition when it comes to golf. You have to beat the competition by knowing the golf course as well as your own skills.

Many lessons are free and offered on your favorite online sites. A lot of times, you can get lessons in acrobat reader formatting and download them onto your PC. They are fairly affordable. However, you need to do the research and compare websites. This will help you to find the most affordable and suitable lessons.

Golf Videos with Instructions

Instructional golfing videos will give great golf lessons, complete with many great graphics that can make your game better. You will get these lessons in real time. They are also available in slow motion where you can look at them over and over again. This will help you to learn at your own pace. Also, there are many different ways to purchase these types of videos as well.

Over time, almost anyone can get better at most sports. It does not matter if you play all the time or just like to play every so often. Eventually, you will know what you can do and what you cannot do. Golf videos can help you to get better at golf in both a mental and physical manner. You will learn all of the latest info about the game of golf.

Also, these types of videos are budget friendly for most people. They are also available on every level of the game. If you need to improve your golf swing, you can watch videos that instruct on how to make improvements to your swing. Watch and analyze at the same time. The instruction is so detailed that you will know exactly what to do and what not to do to in order to achieve the perfect golf swing.

It is easy to find good and cheap instructional videos about golf on the internet. There are known places where you can buy them. You might be able to find a lot of good ones offline as well. Try visiting your local library to find great ones.

Visiting Internet Golf Forums for Tips

If you are looking online for ways to improve your golf game, try going to some of the golfing forums. They offer some really amazing suggestions and resources for improving your game. There are all levels of expertise on these forums. They range from beginners to professionals. All of them have helpful information for your game. Most importantly, there are always reasons for why you should listen to them and try to improve your golf game.

When searching online you will see for yourself that there is plenty of golfing advice available to you. You can visit the many message boards and blogs that are there for you to see. There are all types of people that want to help you. People from all over the world will be happy to give you tips and pointers about golf.

A majority of golf sites are designed to give golfers the latest golfing information available. You can find trending news stories and tips about the game. These sites usually provide links to important information that you will be interested in using.

You can also find tips from professionals who know the ups and downs in golf. You can learn from their mistakes and successes. When you are waiting to tee off, you can use these helpful tips and hit a hole in one for yourself. You will eventually see how these tips improve your game overall. They can change how you play and your overall execution when it comes to golfing.

You will learn all types of things about golf such as etiquette and semantics. You can even brush up on both the mental and physical aspects of the game. Learn from both experts and beginners.

Internet golfing websites have helpful information on golf courses for both pros and novices. Learn all about green fees, golfing seasons or the best golfing locations. Also, did you know that you have the option to play nine holes of golf instead of eighteen? Learn all about golf.

CHAPTER 6: UNDERSTANDING YOUR GOLF CLUBS

The One

Lee Trevino once famously quoted that even God would never be able to hit a one iron. The irony here is that God went on to prove he could hit lots of things, as pro golfer Trevino would eventually be struck by lightning, an even that he thankfully survived.

Of all the bags that you carry in your bag, the one iron is without a doubt the most worthless. Not only is it difficult to hit with, doing it consistently is virtually impossible. This is actually a club that many golfers, the pros included, choose to leave out of the bag completely.

The majority of situations where a golfer might think of using a one iron are situations that are usually better solved by using a wood. For example, a golfer on a par 4 who got halfway to the hole with his drive might very well be able to cover the remaining distance using a one iron. The problem becomes being able to hit the ball as well and as accurately as he would like, which usually means going with a wood, where control is much less of an issue. When playing from the fairway, the three wood is a club that can handle most shots very nicely, and is often used to get the ball on the green in regulation. Simply put, the three wood is a much smarter option than the one iron in most circumstances.

If you insist on having a one iron in the bag, you'll be pleased to know that it works well at dragging out balls that have gone into the water, but are still somewhat reachable.

The Five Iron

If you had to have just one club in your bag, it would likely come down to a toss-up between the five and seven iron. The five iron is a club that is easy to use in a number of different golfing situations.

The seven iron probably offers a little more versatility, but the five is still an excellent club. The angle of the club face means that you can get some loft without having the ball fly on you. It's easy to get the distance you need without overshooting the mark.

The five iron should be pulled out of the bag when you are within two hundred yards of the green. The average golfer can hit a five iron about one hundred and eighty yards, which is still a pretty lengthy approach shot. Despite the fact that you are still a ways out, the five iron is a club that can usually be played with supreme confidence, so easy is it to control. This is a club that will, more often than not, cover the required distance while leaving you nicely set up on the green.

Another situation where the five iron comes in really handy is when you are in the light rough and want to get back on the short stuff. If you are in grass that is starting to creep up into the four to six inch height, you may want to leave the five iron where it is and get the wedge out instead. It's sometimes better to burn a shot than run the risk of raising your frustration level to all new heights.

As already mentioned, control is not really a problem when you use the five iron. You might very well wonder how the five iron has a way of feeling good in your hands and being easy to swing. It all really comes down to comfort with using the club, as most golfers hit this one better than any other. When you have confidence that the club is going to do exactly what you believe it will, you develop a sense of confidence that makes everything seem just right. It is why, without fail, golfers within two hundred yards of the green automatically reach for the five iron.

It is the length of the club that helps make control easy. Hitting the ball correctly with a five iron will usually make the ball land wherever you want it to, making you look like a pro in the process. You can also cover a lot of ground in a few strokes, bringing the cup every closer with each swing.

The Seven Iron

The Kevin Costner movie "Tin Cup" was pure Hollywood, but the use of the seven iron in the flick was not really overstated.

A good golfer could hit the course with nothing but a seven iron and a putter in his bag and still go on to make par. You won't be able to boom the ball down the fairway with a seven iron, but that is not what the club is made for. That said, if you have some strength, you can easily use a seven iron to take off one hundred and seventy five to two hundred and twenty five yard with each and every shot.

If the average golfer were to tee off with a seven iron, the next shot, using the same club, would either be another full swing or a cut down swing, depending on the distance remaining to the green. The prevailing conditions would determine whether the ball would be situated at the front or back of the stance, as that has a direct effect on the amount of loft that the ball will attain when it is struck.

When the ball is closer to the green, the seven iron is able to act as a wedge for chipping the final few yards. Closing up the stance during the swing will result in the ball being flipped onto the short stuff. That said, it is also important to cut the swing to account for distance, otherwise the ball is likely to go sailing right over the green.

The moment the ball lands on the green, the work of the seven iron is over, unless of course you are feeling a little bit adventurous and want to try putting with it. That was a move that Costner pulled in the aforementioned "Tin Cup" movie.

Where the seven iron really comes into play is on short par 3 holes. Again, the golfer can decide where the ball should best be located in his stance. Teeing is also a factor, with a higher tee offering the possibility for grater loft and distance. Having both feet in front of the ball can feel a little odd, but it does prevent too much power being generated, which can cause the ball to sail. This stance will offer a greater level of control when attacking the green.

When a seven iron connects perfectly, the flight of the ball is a joy to behold. It will fly like and arrow and land exactly where you want it to, plopping gently down on the green and leaving you in great shape. This is why the seven iron is such a beloved club.

The 7-Wood

This may very well be the best field wood that you carry in your bag, yet it is also the club that tends to be the most commonly overlooked.

Not everyone is going to agree, but it can be argued that the seven wood is the perfect field wood, and should be considered a must for every bag. The reason it gets those accolades is because it has the easy swinging feel of a six iron, yet offers greater distance and control.

A golfer who has some strength should be able to use this club when situated about two hundred and twenty five yards or closer from the green. The angle of the club makes it easy to get under the ball to generate the loft required to travel that distance. A great little tip here is to try and use a seven wood that has a graphite shaft. This is because the graphite shaft is more flexible than the metal variety, giving better feel and a little more lift when the ball is struck.

The ideal holes for using a seven wood are long par 3's or short par 4's. For example, let's imagine the hole you are on is a par 3 of one hundred and eighty yards. While instinct would make you reach for a three or four iron, using a seven wood offers a little more in the way of options. The ball can be teed up a little higher than normal when the seven wood is used. This allows the ball to get up in the air and on its way to the green that much quicker, especially if the ball was at the back of the stance during set up. All of this will also mean that the swing us reduced, which usually means that the ball will end up not taking an aerial flight up and over the green, resulting in a difficult second shot.

Another great use for a seven wood is to clear an obstacle that might be in the way. Imagine a shot of one hundred and seventy yards, where a tree is situated a mere ten yards away, directly in the path of the upcoming shot. Opening up the stance and putting the hips in a different position can allow you to hook or slice the ball around the tree, but not in such a way that the arc ends up taking the ball even further out of play. This type of shot results in the same type of power and accuracy that the golfer would hope for, whilst also reducing the risk of a worst case scenario result.

The Nine-Iron

While most golfers have a nine iron somewhere in their bag, many of them will be unable to tell you when it should be used.

If you are beyond one hundred and eighty yards from the front of the green, the nine iron should definitely be left in the bag. Anything beyond that distance is usually where the seven or eight iron gets called in. The nine iron has a pretty steeply angled club face, yet it does not hit the same sort of loft you would get from a pitching or sand wedge. That said it can get more distance than any of the clubs that reside in the wedge family of clubs.

This may lead you to wonder what, if anything, the nine iron is good for. Where this club is best served is when it is used as a short-range utility club in situations where you need elevation to get from fairway to green. This is a club that can be used for chipping in a variety of situations, as well as being an adequate sand wedge replacement, if you don't have one of those in your bag.

If you find yourself sitting about one hundred and fifty yards from the green, the nine iron may in fact be a better option than the eight or nine. There is also the option of blading the ball to get more distance, but that would mean giving up on elevation. There are plenty of scenarios where such a shot is required, and where the eight or nine iron is just too much club for the job. Before immediately taking the nine out of the bag, though, you still have to take obstacle and course conditions into account before the next shot is played.

If you find yourself within one hundred yards of the green, the nine iron becomes a very good option. For more elevation, trying putting the ball in the back of the stance, which will also cut down on distance. Keeping the feet closer together when hitting with a nine iron will result in a softer stroke, and will greatly reduce the possibility of flying the green due to a rush of blood to the head.

The nine iron is also a good club when you are facing a short par 3. Depending on the course you are playing, you may come across a par 3 that is one hundred yards or less in length. Going with anything but a nine iron here is folly, although you will still want to pay attention to your stance so as not to overshoot the green. A closed stance is preferred with this type of distance, as the power of the shot, and therefore the distance, will be reduced. This stance will also get the ball up in the air more quickly, and will create a beautiful arc that will gently drop the ball onto the green in the close vicinity of the cup.

That all adds up to the nine iron being a valuable addition to your golf bag.

Drivers

The driver is the name that golfers give to the 1 wood. This is usually the club that dominates the bag in terms of size, as most have a large head. This club is traditionally used for driving on holes that are longer in length. You'd never think of taking out the driver on a short par 3, unless of course your goal is to completely bypass that hole and move on to the next tee box as quickly as possible.

If you are looking to get the ball a long ways down the fairway, this is the club to use. The pros routinely use the driver to hammer the ball distances in excess of three hundred yards. The average golfer will be more likely to get about two hundred and fifty to two hundred and seventy five yards, which is still a nice chunk of yardage to get with that first shot.

As you know, there is no such thing as a set yardage template, with each individual course having its own distances for their holes. You can find a par four that is less than three hundred yards, while others can get up near the five hundred yard range. Whatever the case, you will need to be able to handle a driver well if you want to keep your scores as low as possible.

When driving, distance is key but you also want to have control so that you can steer clear of the hazards that are sure to be in your path.

The Sand and Pitching Wedges

There is more than one wedge to be found when playing golf. The average golf bag usually has several different wedges to choose from, but for now, we will focus on the sand and pitching wedges.

The first thing you will notice is that wedges have handles that are shorter than all the other clubs. The reason for this is to make you get closer to the ball in order for elevation to occur. Height, not distance, is what wedges deliver, which is why they are employed for shots of one hundred yards or less.

If you want to get the ball up in the air as quickly as possible, a pitching wedge is the club for the job. While elevation and not distance is usually what matters with a wedge, you will still want to be sure that you have enough power to get the ball the distance it needs to go to get to the cup.

As the name suggests, the sand wedge is primarily used to get your ball out of sand traps, especially if the trap is around the green. The angle of the club head means that you should not expect the ball to travel any more than around fifty yards. The angle is designed to get the ball up and out of trouble in a hurry, with distance not really a factor.

The sand wedge can be used to get you out of other little jams, though, including using that angled club face to get over trees and back onto the fairway where you belong. If you make the mistake of blading the ball during the shot, there will be no help forthcoming for you. Blading the ball means hitting the ball in the
34

middle, the result of which is a severe decrease in the amount of loft and an increase in distance, both of which are bad in these types of situations. While this is something that can happen with every club, the damaged caused when doing it with a wedge tends to be more severe.

Both the pitching wedge and sand wedge can act as suitable replacements for the pitching wedge. When you have a ball lying in close proximity to the green, you best option is to try and chip it on. Chipping usually takes place when the ball is within one hundred yards of the green, although the further out you are, the more difficult the shot becomes.

If you want to use the sand wedge for chipping, it's best to do so when the ball is about twenty five yards or less from the green. You are looking for loft and a softer touch in these kinds of distances, which is exactly what the sand wedge delivers. The angle of the club face makes it easy to get under the ball, and it won't fly in you too easily.

The pitching wedge is definitely the club to go with in most chipping situations. The amount of loft that you get on the ball when using that club will depend on the positioning of your feet.

CHAPTER 7: HITTING THE BALL

Your feet should be set "X" inches apart, with your body angled ever so slightly to the left. The logo on your shirt should be directly over the ball when you are ready to swing, etc. Directions on how to get into the perfect stance go on and on until they become a total distraction. It is easy to become so consumed with your stance that every other aspect of the game goes out the window. Developing a great game is infinitely more important than developing a great stance. Your ability to enjoy the sport of golf can be severely hampered when you get caught up in all the tiny details.

Does that mean you should ignore your stance completely? Of course not. All the pros will tell you that a good stance and swing are essential ingredients in a god golf game. A less than perfect stance may still result in a great drive, but working on that stance will help you develop a golf game that is consistently good.

The first thing you need to do is learn how to relax. This is often easier said than done, especially when you are first starting out and your brain is filled with all the little details that make up a great stance. You should have you arms in a fixed position, but they should not be rigid. Golf coaches often get new players to start with their arms relaxed by their side.

Many different factors come into play with the stance, including the gender of the golfer. It is generally agreed that female golfers should have a wider stance than men. It is the stance that is the biggest building block of the swing, which means balance is crucial. When you consider that the hips and pelvis size of women and men are naturally different, you can see how their stances would have to differ. The hips of the male golfer are generally more rigid than the female, which means their body will have a different reaction to the counter swing and follow through. Women actually have a bit of an edge when it comes to the stance, as they have hips that naturally swing more easily. Practice your stance until you find the position that feels most natural to you.

It is important that you are comfortable in your stance, although you may need to compromise on that a little to get it just right. This does not mean that you should develop a stance that is truly painful, but you may have to learn to live with a little discomfort until your body grows accustomed to the stance you are developing. Make sure that your muscles are loosened up before you hit the course, and take time to practice as you make adjustments.

While the stance is only a single element in your entire game, it's an important one. When you combine a great stance with a solid grip and swing, you are usually left with a consistent golf game. Before you decide to get all caught up in the dynamics of the stance, remember that the game is supposed to be fun. If you find that fretting about the stance is sucking all of your enjoyment out of playing golf, it may be time to re-evaluate what a successful golf game means to you.

Golfing in the Wind

The elements can greatly affect your golf game, with the wind often the most disruptive. A soggy course will mean that your ball won't travel as far as normal, but the wind can make it tough to even get the ball up in the air at all. As such, the wind can greatly affect the outcome of your round.

This happens because a strong gust of wind can very easily divert your ball from its intended path, oftentimes dropping it in spots that are less than perfect.

It is worth remembering that the majority of golfers play right-handed, which is why we will be focusing the wind discussion from a right-handed player's perspective. The first thing the golfer should be aware of is the direction in which the wind is blowing. This is, of course, under regular windy conditions, as all bets can be considered off when a gale is howling across the fairway. In those types of conditions, having any sort of directional control over the ball becomes almost impossible. The only difference is when the wind is blowing from behind, as that is when you want to get the ball in the air and let the wind work in your favor.

Let's imagine you step into the tee box and are buffeted by a wind going from right to left. It's a relatively short par 3, with the hole located about 150 yards from the tee box and the flag right in the middle of the green. If you aim directly at the flag, you will likely be disappointed when your ball shoots off to the left of the hole. If there is a severe slope on the green, that landing spot can mean that your ball rolls off the short stuff completely. You will then be forced to try and save par with a delicate up and down chip shot and putt. None of this would happen if the wind was taken into account before the first shot was played.

Let's take it up a notch and assume that the golfer is at a par 4, three hundred and ninety five yard hold with the wind blowing in his face. The best shot a golfer can play in these conditions is to alter his stance and hit a shot where the call stays low. This move will help him hit a decent drive. The same rules apply with the approach shot that follows, once again getting into a stance that will keep the ball low. The best way to achieve this is to select a club that is one larger than what would traditionally be played with no wind present. For example, if the gold would routinely choose a 7-iron for a shot of about one hundred and fifty yards, he or she would then move to a 5 or 6-iron when the wind is in their face.

Putting Done Right

The vast majority of golfers devote most of their practice time to driving. It's somewhat understandable, as nothing looks as good as a well struck ball heading right up the middle of the fairway. The only thing better may in fact be the sound of the ball dropping into the cup, which is something that can only be achieved with a good putting stroke.

A great putting stroke is something that takes time and practice to master. It's also essential that you do, as hitting the green in regulation is only great if you can finish it all off with a great putt. Read on to see what the pros have to say about putting.

One of the biggest fears of a golfer is developing a case of the "yips." This is a hesitation when putting that is akin to a hiccup. Since the perfect putt depends on a smooth stroke, any type of hesitation is considered a bit of a disaster.

Accuracy is important when you practice putting. If you are constantly having a problem in controlling the line of travel, try adding some little helpers. Placing a mark on your club may help you find the center of the putter more easily. Marking the ball is another thing that the pros use to perfect the swing. If you are concerned about marking up all your balls, try using chalk, as this is easy to clean off once practice is over.

Paint a picture in your mind of the path that the ball needs to follow to the cup. If that doesn't work, use string to create a path from the ball to the cup. While that may seem like an overly simplistic method, it can help you see where you are going wrong when the ball starts to deviate from its intended path.

Putting too much spin on the ball can create some real problems. Pros will tell you that spin is incredibly difficult to control, yet it is control that is at the heart of a great putt.

If you are left with a long putt, remember that you don't have to muscle the ball to the hole. Creating any sort of loft in these situations will quickly out the ball out of control.

There may also be the temptation to overshoot the hole, but that also needs to be avoided. This is a problem that is actually quite common in a number of different sports, with the likes of pool, football, baseball, and more all falling prey to players overshooting the mark. Overshooting can make your situation worse, as you next putt may end up being even longer than the one that you just hit. That is why controlling the amount of power you use when putting is essential to getting it just right.

When you are over the ball and ready to putt, take a moment to think about control and using just the right amount of power.

Navigating the Golf Traps

There is nothing worse than getting all of the basic elements of the game down pat, only to end up buried in a sand trap or stuck behind the largest tree on the golf course. No matter how good your game is, you are going to run into these scenarios a few times in every round. The reality is that if there were no rough, sand traps, water hazards, or trees, the game of golf might not be as challenging or fun. As frustrating as they can be, obstacles actually play a pretty big role in making the game of golf so much fun to play. The key to enjoying the game I knowing how to navigate all of those traps.

When your ball rolls up behind a tree, you may think that you are seriously out of options. While chopping down the tree would do the trick, it is not really practical or acceptable. Instead, you simply have to realize your predicament and sacrifice a shot.

What that means is that you will simply putt or chip the ball back onto the fairway where you will have a much easier lie. Yes, it will have essentially cost you a shot, but having a clear shot next time helps take away a lot of the frustration you are likely feeling.

It is often frustration that causes golfers to pull the sand wedge out of the bag and just blast way at a ball that has landed in a bunker. In these cases, it is often the sand that travels further than the ball, which may very well still be in the sand trap.

The key to a good golf game is playing consistently, even when faced with obstacles. Getting out of the sand can be tricky indeed, especially when you know that you have to chip out, and that the upward face of the trap means getting enough loft to clear the obstacle and get out. Instead of trying to muscle your way out, choose the wedge you need and take a nice even stroke, making sure that you have the control required to get the loft that is needed to clear the face of the trap.

Keep in mind what we said about the need for control, which often means choosing a wedge with less loft, as control is easier with that type of club.

Just like any shot in golf, the obstacle shot requires choosing the best club, getting your stance correct, and using a controlled swing to get the best results.

CHAPTER 8: GOLF SOFTWARE

Understanding the basics of playing golf is something that is best done "hands on." That said there are other teaching methods that can help you to understand the basic components of the games, whilst also helping you improve your skills. If you really want to take your golf skills to the next level, software may help you do it. You may in fact be more than a little surprised at just how many benefits you can get from using golf learning software.

The best instructional golf software on the market can be used by amateur golfers, as well as those that have made it to the professional ranks. All of the information shown on the software is presented and formatted in a way that is easy for everyone to understand. The instructions can be delivered in different levels and at different price points so that anyone who loves to swing a club can take advantage of what's on offer.

The only way that you can truly evaluate how good any piece of software has been is by looking at how much your game improves after using it. All of the best golf websites will deliver the pros and cons of all the instructional software out there, as well as links that will take you to free trial downloads. The great thing about being able to give the software a test run is to see whether the level of instruction that is included is suitable for your game and skill level.

While you may feel that newer software, which has a number of technological advancements included, might be the best, there are still plenty of older software versions that can get the job done, too. The reality is that while golf is a fun game to participate in, the only way to get the most out of it and improve as you go along, a few lessons will be required.

As is the case with any sport, there are some people who are just naturals. They are small in number, though, with everyone else needing some sort of guidance and instruction in order to improve and get a better sense of the game. That part of the game has little to do with your overall proficiency, but what it does do is help you to figure out which aspects of the game you are competent at, and which need some more work.

Golf is one game that is as much a challenge against yourself as well as against others. You have to overcome individual challenges in order to be victorious against your friends. Having software that can help you with every aspect of the game is an incredible tool to have at your disposal. Choosing the software that is correct for you really isn't that difficult to do.

Improve Your Game with Golf Swing Analysis Software

One of the quickest ways to improve your game and bring your score down is to focus on improving your swing. The good news is that there are a large number of instructional videos and software out there that can help you achieve that. Even the professionals take time to have their swing evaluated so that they can spot potential weaknesses that can be improved upon.

Your swing can definitely be improved by looking objectively at your technique and style. Modern instructional golf software will help you analyze your swing, but there are also plenty of older titles that have proven to be effective for long periods of time and which are still used to this day.

There is golf swing analysis software out there for golfers of all different skill levels. Even if you only get out on the course once or twice a month, your swing can be vastly improved by using the analysis the software provides. That will help improve your overall game, too.

Some of the software out there will include instruction from respected golf pros. There will also be software that features regular everyday golfers like yourself, allowing you to compare you swing against theirs.

Software of this type is very easy to find and download, and is even easier to use. You may in fact be able to get your hands on a free trial version so that you can narrow down the search and find the one that is best for your specific needs.

The tools that are now used to analyze golf swings – slow motion camera capture and virtual comparison – are incredibly advanced, yet there are still versions out there that can fit the budget of just about every golfer.

Golf is a sport that is very much on the rise in popularity, thanks in large part to how often it is now shown on TV. What connects golfers who have been playing for years with those who are new to the game is that they want to find ways to improve. The latest software can help you do that in a relatively short period of time.

Tracking Your Golf Handicap with Software

All of the top golfers have a handicap that has been pretty well documented, with most amateur golfers setting that as the number they want to achieve. Keeping track of the handicap for the amateur golfer can be a real chore, but technology has made it easier.

There are both software and online handicapping options that will help your track your handicap, and will even keep track of your scores so that you can get your handicap together for tournaments.

There are a wide variety of options available that can get you what you need, no matter what type of budget you are working with. You can spend less than $20, or go for more sophisticated software that comes in at over $100.

What the programs deliver is as wide and varied as the prices they charge. You can choose a piece of software that does all of the numerical calculations for you and creates a spreadsheet of stats, or you can go with something that gives you a simple handicap number.

The one thing that you need to remember is that the software you choose will only work as well as your record-keeping skills. If you don't have a lot of time to fit smaller tasks into your schedule, you may discover that you simply don't have the time or patience to accurately record your data into the software. That said a great piece of software may be all the motivation you need to get you working towards an improved handicap.

One of the major benefits that online handicapping tools have over software is that you can enter in the data anytime, and often from any type of device. That allows you to enter your numbers the moment your round is over.

There are some real benefits to keeping track of your handicap, even if you are only a casual golfer who doesn't get to play that often. You may feel as though you are making the great shots, but seeing the improvement in your handicap will show that the improvements are in fact real.

CHAPTER 9: WHAT IS THE IDEAL GOLF COURSE?

Most people want to know what makes a golf course a world class golf course. Basically, it is all about the location.

An ideal golf course has to have a couple of ponds, hills, trees and land that is good enough for a fairway. Unfortunately, it also has to have spots that aren't as inviting. These are perfect places to put sand traps. Amazingly, there are golfers who think that golf courses should not have sand traps, but they are incorrect and clearly not in the majority. Quite frankly, sand traps add more depth to the game. It makes the game challenging, which motivates golfers to hone in on their skills.

Each hole of a great golf course must be different and entertaining. If every hole was the same, the game would not be exciting. The best golf courses have holes that dogleg left and right. It should have a lot of challenges so that it is hard to see the flag from the tee box.

The best golf courses have elevated tees, which help golfers to have elevated drives. When the ball gets to the fairway, how high it goes will depend on how skilled the golfer really is.

An ideal golf course has a wonderful crew that keeps it looking great. A lot of golf courses hire professionals to keep the grounds looking good. The fairways must remain smooth, the sand traps challenging and the grounds landscaped. These are the types of things that really make or break a golf course for many golfers. The same thing can be said about the kind of grass that is used.

When it comes to the grass that is normally used, an ideal golf course should have bent grass greens. This type of grass won't let the ball roll off of the green once it lands. Although it is considered to be premium grass, Bermuda grass doesn't have the ability to stop the speed of the golf ball when it lands. Obviously, bend grass will have more divots than Bermuda grass because the ground is usually not as hard.

The work ethic of the ground crew will determine if a golf course is ideal. If the workers don't care about how a golf course looks, then you probably aren't going to care much about it either. A happy golfing crew has the ability to make your overall golfing experience very relaxing and entertaining.

An ideal golf course has well maintained golf paths too. A bad golf course path will make golfers want to walk on the fairways instead. Although this might not seem like a bad thing, it is very frustrating for the groundskeepers.

However, one of the things that make a golf course bad is rough terrain. Things such as the terrain and rocks tend to have a bad impact on how golf balls land and roll.

The Games are Different, But not the Course

No two golf courses are ever alike. You could go and play on different courses, but playing on your home course will always be a fun and gruelling game. It does not matter how many times you do it because each time there will be different variables.

Yes, you are playing on the same home course. It remains the same except for maybe how it is cut or manicured each time. However, there will always be something different about the golf course that you play on each and every day.

In the movie "The Legend of Bagger Vance," one of the main characters says that the grass on a course follows the sun. So, this means that every morning the grass will be different from the way that it is in the afternoon.

Another thing that makes your favorite golf course different every day has to do with the weather. Weather has a huge impact on your game of golf and the course that you play on. If you play after a heavy rain goes through the area, your game will be slow because the ball does not land the way that it normally does. Obviously, a ball rolls a further distance when the ground is dry.

If the weather is hot, the game will be different from a game that is played in cold weather. The ball does not travel as fast in cold weather. On the flip side, if you hit the same ball on a hot day, it will travel much further. Also, if the weather has been dry within recent days, the ball will go even further since the ground is hard.

Obviously, your attitude will affect the way that you play. When playing the game of golf, you have to be cool and concentrate heavily on what you are doing.

Another thing that will affect your game is how well thé grounds are maintained. A long fairway will hinder the golf ball from rolling a longer distance. If the grounds are kept short, then the ball will travel a greater distance.

There are other things that can affect your game such as "the rough" and sprinkler heads. You can expect the rough to be difficult to play on, but this is even more of a problem if it is wet. You'll probably take a longer time to chip away at the ball in order to get back on the fairway. Quite naturally, the ball never does what you want it to do if it keeps hitting sprinkler heads.

In addition, your golf game is affected by whether or not you are playing along or with others. Also, if you are accustomed to playing with others and have to play alone, this will impact your game too. So, this is another example of how the same golf course can lead to many different types of games and outcomes due to various factors.

Stimp Meters: How fast is the Course?

A lot of new golfers are unfamiliar with stimp meters. Chances are if you are not a pro, you may never need one. However, understand that a stimp meter is important if you are concerned about the speed of the golf course. So, you might want to become knowledgeable about stimp meters.

Thus, after you have played golf for a while, you will hear other golfers say that the course is stimping. This indicates how fast the course is running. You can tell the speed by using a stimp meter.

A stimp meter is utilized to determine how fast the course is running. You can calculate this by rolling the ball down the meter in eight differing directions. The average distance of the ball when it touches the course is the stimp rating. For example, if the ball rolls about 12 feet when it gets on the course, then it has a stimp rating of 12. A higher number means that the course is running faster. The average public golf course has a stimp rating in the range of seven to ten.

What is the big deal about a stimp rating? Although it may never come in handy unless you are a pro and have competitors, this rating could tell you why you had a horrible game of golf. For example, a good game on a course that has an average rating is a good thing. But, you might not do so well on a course that has a higher stimp rating.

When using the stimp rating, make sure that you take into consideration whether or not you are playing on artificial or real grass. It was once said that there was a difference in the rating when playing on natural grass as opposed to artificial grass. But, this really is not a problem these days. Most manufacturers have turf that that is designed with natural blends, so it looks and feels like genuine grass. Basically, you should not have any problems with your stimp rating when playing on artificial grass.

If you want to practice in your own backyard, then purchase an artificial putting green. If you want to practice based upon your favorite golf course, then just change the stimp rating when you are practicing. Find out which companies have the best artificial putting green before you make your final decision. There will be benefits for each of them, so do your research before purchasing an artificial putting green.

If you just want to play a relaxing game of golf and aren't really worried about the speed of the course, then you might not have to learn about stimp ratings. If you are fine with the speed of the golf course, then don't worry about it. But, at least learn as much as you can about a stimp rating so that you will know what the pros are talking about when they say that a particular golf course is "stimping."

CHAPTER 10: DESCRIBE THE PERFECT GOLF OUTING

How would you describe the perfect golf outing? There are probably zillions of different answers to this question because nobody is the same, and everyone probably has more than one answer to this question.

Maybe you want to play pro golfers and on one of the big golf courses. What serious golfer hasn't ever dreamed about playing at the Masters or U.S Open? Many would give anything to experience this opportunity at least once during their lifetime. These are golf courses where the best in golf have played. People such as Arnold Palmer and Tiger Woods have graced these golf courses. Yes, Tiger Woods might be young, but he is still considered to be one of the best in the game.

Or, maybe your perfect golf outing has more to do with the location. It is all about the weather instead. Some golfers like to play in mild climates that have cool breezes. But, others want to play in extreme weather conditions. They consider this to be more of a challenge. Then there are those who are extremely adventurous and want to play when the temperatures are burning up or freezing. Amazingly, they just want to be able to prove that they can play in these harsh weather conditions.

But on the other hand, maybe your perfect golf outing does not involve any of the aforementioned things. You just want to play on a fun golf course with your best friends. It's all about playing a good game of golf and enjoying the company of your friends. Surprisingly, you are not alone when it comes to describing your perfect golf outing. Most people feel the same way that you do. They like to play in groups or as couples. Sure, you are probably teased when you miss a shot, but then everyone in your party praises you when you get a wonderful shot as well. When it comes down to it, the final score is not important, unless there is a bet on the game. But, even that is done all in fun. The most important thing is that the outing is remembered for the fun and laughter that is shared. It is a wonderful way for good friends to get together, relieve stress and have a little fun together.

CHAPTER 11: THE GAME OF GOLF: RELAXING, HONORABLE AND VERY POPULAR

Golf has really grown in popularity. Many golfers claim that they cannot live without playing the game. But, on the other hand, they also say that it takes a lot of effort and discipline to play the game. As time goes on, you will know how a seven iron and seven wood are different. You will know when to use the iron and how to get out of sand traps. Even though these are obvious lessons, golfing also has a lot of techniques and strategies that aren't as obvious.

However, technology has greatly influenced the game. Now it is possible to get the speed of a golf course just by utilizing a stimp meter. You can also monitor your golfing scores via software and know your handicap. It is also possible to find software packages that tell what you are doing so that you can make corrections to your golfing swing.

The golf industry is big money. There are manufacturers that make all types of cutting edge golfing equipment from balls to clubs. There are a lot of people that give golf lessons for a living. There are also plenty of schools that offer week long programs that will show you how to play the game and get rid of bad golfing habits. They can teach you how to get a better grip and stance. Golfing involves more effort than learning how to drive the ball. You also have to know how to put, watch the ball and stay in top physical shape as well. This is what golfing is all about.

Golf is a very diverse game and this is obvious by watching the people that play the game. Any type of person can play golf if they are in shape physically. It is a good way to get in some needed exercise while in the great outdoors. It is a game where you can exercise and be in a relaxing setting. This is because most golf courses are very beautiful and appealing. And the best part is that you don't have to be rich to play the game. Golf is no longer considered a game for just the privileged. So, it should not be surprising to learn that many courses are public and budget friendly.

It does not matter if you are a man or woman. The game is competitive for both genders. But, keep in mind that the game is not mean spirited. In addition to having fierce competitors, you will also have to deal with gruelling golf courses and unaccommodating weather. However, the biggest challenge that most golfers face involves trying to get better at the game.

Finally, golf is also all about honor. This should not shock you. Besides, golf is the only game where you can give yourself a penalty. Well, the honourable players have been known to do this. But, there are those that would never give themselves and penalty, even though they consider themselves to be wonderful golfers. They don't get high scores in golf. Thus, it should not surprise anyone that they get low scores in their everyday lives too.

Don't forget that golfing is so magnificent that the worst day on the golf course is considered to be better than the best day in the office.

MEET THE AUTHOR

Aaron Knight grew up a military brat and has lived in numerous places including Germany, Texas, Georgia, Alaska, Hawaii and California. Aaron is an avid golf player who started playing the game as a teenager and immediately fell in love with this sport. Over the past fifteen years Aaron has taken to many golf lessons to keep track of, invested in custom golf clubs, played in tournaments, played on PGA courses and conducted business transactions on the greens. Aaron tees up on average 3-to-four times per week.

Aaron has taken his golf experience and knowledge to write his debut book *Golf Basics for Beginners*. Aaron hopes to encourage others who are interested in golf sort through terminology, equipment, etiquette, etc., that are necessary to understand in this challenging, frustrating (at times) but fun sport.

Aaron currently resides in Idaho with his wife and daughter. When not playing golf Aaron enjoys hunting, camping, 4-wheeling and fine cigars.